D1400352

Step-by-Step Dividend Investing

A Beginner's Guide to the Best Dividend Stocks and Income Investments

Joseph Hogue

About this Book

Over the 15 years through 2014, stocks in the S&P 500 lost money a third of the time with investors losing an average of 16% when the market tumbled.

Even on gains in other years, investors earned an annualized return of just 2.3% over the period…that's barely enough to cover inflation.

But one group of stocks has consistently beaten the rest of the market. **In fact, this group has provided a source for positive returns every single year – without fail.**

Even when the prices of dividend stocks fall, the regular stream of cash they provide is a constant source for positive returns.

One group of dividend stocks has jumped 314% over that same 15-year period, providing more than twice the return you would have gotten from the general market.

After reading this book, you'll know exactly how to take advantage of returns on dividend stocks and how to build a portfolio around income investments.

This book is the second in a series of four, outlining a step-by-step process for a simple investing strategy. In this book about investing in stocks that regularly put money in your pocket, I start off by showing you the power of dividend investing.

After talking about the three income investments everyone needs in their portfolio, I'll show you how to put together an investing plan that will benefit from a regular stream of cash and upside price appreciation.

In this book you'll learn:

- The four reasons why everyone needs to own dividend stocks and how they can help you reach financial freedom. (pg. 8)

- One group of dividend stocks that outperformed the stock market by 100% over the last decade. (pg. 22)

- The real estate dividend investment that has returned 13% a year for four decades. (pg. 24)

- The reason most investors lose money and a simple four-step process for investing in dividend stocks. (pg. 40)

Check out the other three books in the Step-by-Step Investing series to round out your investing strategy. You'll get everything you need to lay out a sleep-at-night investing strategy that will meet your financial goals.

I've put nearly a decade of work as an investment analyst into the series and hope you can use it to develop a simple strategy that will meet your goals. If you find the ideas useful, *please leave a review on Amazon* to let others know.

Joseph Hogue, CFA

Born and raised in Iowa, Joseph Hogue graduated from Iowa State University after serving in the Marine Corps. He worked in corporate finance and real estate before starting a career in investment analysis. Mr. Hogue has appeared on Bloomberg as an expert in emerging market investing and has led a team of equity analysts for sell-side research. His investment analysis has been featured in advisor newsletters, institutional research reports and in the financial press.

He holds the Chartered Financial Analyst (CFA) designation, the gold standard for ethical and professional conduct in investment management.

PeerFinance101.com is a new kind of personal finance blog where readers share their own stories of personal finance challenges and success. There's no one-size-fits-all solution to meeting your financial goals but you'll find a lot of similarities in others' stories and a lot of ideas that will help you get through your own challenges.

Click through to PeerFinance101 for topics from investing to managing debt as well as retirement planning and frugal living.

Step-by-Step Dividend Investing: A Beginner's Guide to the Best Dividend Stocks and Income Investments

ISBN-13 (eBook) 978-0-9962321-6-6
ISBN-13 (Print) 978-0-9962321-7-3

Contents

Income Investing and Your Path to Financial Freedom

Is it any surprise that dividend stocks have been one of the most popular investing strategies since the first payment was made to owners of the Dutch East India Company over 400 years ago?

While investing in other stocks may offer the dream of getting rich when the investment is sold, regular dividends put cash in your pocket that you can spend or reinvest.

Two major stock market crashes in less than a decade have made dividend investing even more popular and more necessary. Investors have seen their price appreciation wiped out multiple times with dividends being the only remaining value.

With interest rates at historic lows and bonds paying almost nothing after inflation, investors have also found new hope for income in shares of companies with healthy dividend yields.

Dividend investing may just be one of the only true paths to financial freedom. The safety and reliability of dividends turn you into an owner, collecting income off the assets, rather than simply a tenant of other people's assets.

In this first chapter, we'll cover the principal advantages of dividend investing before getting into the definition and process of collecting dividends. We'll wrap it up with a brief look at the different types of dividend investments.

The four principal advantages of dividend investing:

- Powerful returns on compound interest

- Ability to reduce inflation risk

- Safety when the stock market crashes

- An income stream and financial freedom!

The Power of Dividend Stocks and Compounding Returns

Maybe the strongest evidence in favor of dividend investing is the actual return in the market. The graph below shows the annual compound return to four groups of stocks in the 37 years to 2010.

Shares of companies that paid dividends but did not regularly raise their payments provided investors with a 7.1% annual return over the period, well above the 1.8% annual return from companies that paid no dividends.

But companies that regularly increased their dividend payments did even better, returning an average 9.3% a year over nearly four decades!

In dollar terms, if you had invested $10,000 to a portfolio of dividend growth stocks in 1973, by 2010 you would have more than $268,500 in your account.

Compare that to $126,500 in the portfolio of companies that paid dividends without regular payment increases and just $19,350 in the portfolio of non-dividend paying stocks.

The outperformance of dividend-paying stocks makes sense on a financial level. For a company to pay dividends, it must make a detailed projection of its cash flow and plan sometimes years in advance for sales and growth projects.

Once a dividend is set, a company dare not cut the payment for the signal of weakness it sends to investors. For this reason, a dividend payment is a limitation on the use of cash and helps discipline management.

Free cash flow is like a narcotic to management, clouding their judgment and often leading to overconfidence. Management sees all the money rolling in and starts to think about building their legacy through pet projects, executive perks, and billion-dollar acquisitions. A high and increasing dividend payment keeps management grounded and limits the amount of trouble they can get into.

With management constrained by the dividend, they're only able to go with the most profitable projects and have to think twice before giving themselves massive bonuses and perks.

An Alternative to Low Interest Rates and an Inflation Hedge

The Ten-year Treasury bond, the instrument against which all other bonds are priced, hit a record low of 1.39% in 2012. Inflation that year increased by 1.7% so the U.S. government was actually charging investors a third of a percent to hold their money each year over the next decade.

To me, that doesn't sound like any way to meet your financial goals!

Since the market uses the rate paid on risk-free treasuries to price other bonds, the yields on all fixed-income investments have come down to the point that you'd have trouble meeting investment goals with a portfolio of bonds.

Even corporate bonds only pay a 2.6% yield after accounting for inflation and with no prospect for price appreciation if held to maturity.

Dividend investing has come to the rescue for many people living off the income from their investments.

A lot of dividend-paying companies have been in business so long, they are nearly as safe an investment as the U.S. government. Some even have a better credit rating!

Since companies are generally able to increase prices along with inflation, dividend stocks offer a protection against inflation that you won't find in bonds. Bonds lose their value with inflation and higher interest rates while dividend stocks hold up and even increase in value.

Besides the tendency for dividend payments to increase with inflation, there are several groups of dividend stocks that offer additional protection against rising prices. Utility companies, the classic defensive dividend stocks, are sometimes contractually allowed to raise the rate on their services by an inflation adjustment. The adjustment may lag a year or two but will even out over many years and compensate for higher prices.

But isn't inflation dead? Prices rose just 0.8% last year and have averaged just 1.7% over the last five. Before you shrug off the need to protect your assets against the loss of purchasing power, take a look at the graphic below.

Value of the U.S. Dollar, 1960 - 2012

Source: Federal Reserve Economic Data

Even at a low rate of 2.0% inflation, the value of your money halves in 34 years. Imagine getting to retirement and your money buys half as much as you were expecting.

Low inflation over the last decade may be the exception rather than the rule. In the 30 years to 2000, the average annual rate of inflation was 5.2%, more than double its current rate. Tack on historic programs of monetary stimulus by central banks all over the world and you've got a recipe for higher prices in the future.

While we may not see the 7.1% rate of inflation experienced in the 70s, we are likely to see rates closer to 3% over the next several decades.

At a moderate 3% annual rise in prices, your dollar is worth just two-thirds of its value in 10 years and it takes just 23 years to halve its value.

Yield provides safety net in market downturn

For me, all the data on dividends and market-beating returns is just icing on the cake. Like many investors, dividend stocks are my 'sleep-at-night investments.' Studies show that dividend-paying stocks are less sensitive to market changes and outperform the general market even more when stock prices come down.

Over the two decades to 2012, dividend-paying stocks within the S&P 500 posted an annualized return of 11.3% against 10.4% for stocks that paid no dividends. Again, icing on the cake but the dividend-payers also did it with lower risk and volatility in prices.

Shares of stocks that paid no dividends were 20% riskier than dividend-paying stocks over the period. Not only did the dividend-payers beat the non-paying stocks by nearly a percentage point on an annual basis, but they did it with much less risk.

While stock prices may rise or fall in any given year, dividend returns will always be positive. That dividend check is money in the bank and can't be taken away even if stock prices collapse. Over the 85 years to 2012, stocks in the S&P 500 increased an average of 24% on up years with 5% of that from dividends. During years where stock prices fell, the average loss was 15% but dividend payments still offered a positive 3% return.

When the market is rising, returns to dividend investing are good and adds to total returns. When the market is falling, returns to dividend investing are great and can cushion you from bigger losses and panic-selling.

Dividend Stocks for Income and Financial Freedom

Finally, dividend investing provides a stable source of income for millions of Americans.

Americans are increasingly relying on dividend income for their everyday needs. Data from the Bureau of Economic Analysis shows wages and dividends as percentages of total personal income over the three decades to 2013. Wages and salaries have sunk to just half of total personal income while dividend payments have grown to more than 5% of the total.

In fact, more than $757 billion was collected from dividend payments in 2012.

Distribution of Personal Income (percentage of total, 1983 - 2013)

Source: Bureau of Economic Analysis

If you look at the graph not as the personal income of the country but as a representation of your own income, one other thing becomes clear about dividends...

Dividends are your path to financial freedom.

As a young investor, you are relying heavily on your salary to pay the bills and dividend income is probably relatively small. Over the years, as your portfolio grows, dividend income grows and becomes a larger part of your total income. Dividend investing can help you reach the financial freedom to depend less on wages and more on the fruits of your labor.

What are dividends?

Running a company is a constant choice between growing the business and taking hard-earned profits. If profits are used to invest in more equipment and other business necessities, they could lead to more profits in the future. Profits paid out to the owners may not add to business growth but they're the ultimate reason for creating and running that business.

A dividend is those profits paid out to the owners of the business. While small companies may just have one or a few owners, very large companies raise money through selling shares and distributing the ownership over thousands of owners.

The decision to return profits or invest in the business isn't necessarily an either/or decision. Most successful businesses make enough each year to return a little bit of profit as well as invest in future growth.

For most companies, dividends are paid every three months according to a fixed amount for every share you own. There are companies that pay dividends twice or once a year, or even twelve times a year but these are the exception rather than the rule.

Most companies pay a fairly constant dividend because many investors depend on that cash flow for living expenses. For this reason, management often plans several years in advance to make sure they'll have the money to pay for growth projects and a consistent or rising dividend.

Besides regular cash dividends, a company may find itself with excess cash that it no longer needs. In this case, the Board might approve a 'special' or one-time dividend payment. The process of paying out this dividend is the same but it is usually much larger than the regular dividend payments.

How the process of paying a dividend works

The Board of Directors is a group of people elected to represent you as an owner of the company. When management decides it will have sufficient cash for growth projects, the Board of Directors votes to declare and pay a dividend. The entire process includes four important dates.

The **declaration date** is the day the dividend is announced by the company to the public. On this date, the company will also announce a date of record and payment date for the dividend.

The **date of record** is the date that determines which shareholders will actually receive the dividend.

The **ex-dividend date** is the first day that the stock trades without the dividend. This means, anyone that did not own the shares prior to this day will not receive the dividend payment. In a confusing twist, the ex-dividend date is usually before the date of record. This is because of the time it takes for share ownership to actually be recorded with the company, usually two business days.

For example, if the date of record for a dividend payment in shares of McDonald's (MCD) is on Friday, the ex-dividend date will likely be on Wednesday of that week. If you sold your shares on Wednesday, you would still receive the dividend payment because your sale would not be recorded with the company until after the date of record when it has determined who gets the payment.

The **payment date** is the day you will see the dividend appear in your account according to the amount and how many shares you own. For example, if you own 100 shares of the Coca-Cola Company (KO) and the company pays a $0.30 quarterly dividend then you will receive $30 on the payment date.

Distributions versus Dividends

Another important distinction in the money you get back from your stocks is that of distributions versus dividends. Many people use the terms interchangeably but there is an important difference.

Dividends are a return of shareholder cash declared by a company. Distributions, most often paid by Real Estate Investment Trusts (REITs) and Limited Partnerships (LPs), are a return of equity in the company. A return of equity (or ownership) is management saying that it does not need quite as much capital and is returning part of the company's assets to the owners.

You pay taxes every year on dividends, whether at the capital gains rate or as income. You are not taxed on distributions each year. The amount of distributions you collect are deducted from the original price you paid for the shares. When you sell the shares, you pay taxes on the difference between the selling price and the new, lower price you paid for the shares.

Distributions may increase the taxes you owe when you sell the shares but may not be due for many years depending on how long you hold the investment. Being able to pay taxes later on money today is a great advantage of stocks that pay out distributions as well as dividends.

Types of dividend stocks and Income Investments

There are more than 800 publicly listed companies that trade on the New York Stock Exchange, Nasdaq and the American Stock Exchange that pay dividends. In fact, the list of dividend-paying stocks is so large and diverse that your biggest challenge is going to be choosing the best for your portfolio.

Fortunately, dividend stocks can be categorized to narrow the field of options for your own investment needs. The groups are not exclusive, so some companies may be in multiple categories but the list will be a good start to thinking about different options.

The table shows the dividend yield, average annual return over the last decade and the risk on some popular income investments.

	Current Income Yield	Average Annual Return	Risk
MLPs	9.4%	8.7%	14%
Corporate Bonds	4.6%	6.2%	9%
REITs	4.1%	8.1%	24%
Dividend Stocks	3.5%	7.4%	19%
10-Year Treasury	2.6%	3.7%	6%
S&P 500	2.2%	7.1%	21%

Source: Bloomberg, Yahoo Finance

The return and risk on these income investments will differ from year-to-year and the chart shouldn't be used as a plan to load up on those with the biggest returns. We'll cover dividend stocks, MLPs and REITs separately in different chapters.

Besides the dividend investing plan we'll cover in this book, you might want to check out two others in the series. Step-by-Step Bond Investing will show you how to add fixed-income investments to your investing plan to reduce your risk while still putting money in your pocket.

While stocks of companies in developing countries are not listed in the table, most pay extremely attractive dividend yields. Check out Step-by-Step Emerging Market Investing to learn how to add stocks of companies in fast-growing markets to your plan.

While dividend stocks offer a lower income yield than corporate bonds, they offer the opportunity for price gains as well. Bond prices may decline sharply on higher interest rates, eating into the dividend yield. Bond prices fell in 2014 and investors lost money while dividend stocks saw their investment surge by more than 20% over the year.

Not only do dividend stocks pay a higher yield than stocks across the general market (S&P 500) but they have a higher total return and do it with less risk!

While I'll talk about the advantages and weaknesses in different income investments throughout the book, you'll see in the step-by-step process that the best plan is one that combines almost all the investment options. Combining the high yields and relatively low risk from dividend stocks, MLPs, REITs and bonds can help smooth out market fluctuations and provide strong and stable income.

Dividend Stocks: Putting Cash in Your Pocket

Can I say that I love dividend-paying stocks too many times in this book? I haven't always been the smartest investor, investing in my 20s and falling into the same traps that lose money for most people. I would buy and sell into hot stocks or overcomplicated strategies and then get disappointed when I didn't 'beat' the market.

But my dividend stocks always provided a stable return. Besides the better return on dividend stocks overall, I think there's another reason why investors do so well with companies that pay out a constant stream of cash.

Unlike hot growth stocks touted in the market, most dividend-paying companies are older and in mature industries. This means you're less likely to look at them as get-rich-quick investments, instead buying them for the long-term. This perspective helps to avoid jumping in and out of stocks, paying mountains of fees and losing money on market-timing.

We'll start this chapter by looking at some popular ways to group dividend stocks and some basic analysis for picking the best investments. We're going to reinforce that idea of 'basic' analysis and simplicity throughout the book.

Over a decade as an investment analyst, I've found that the most basic strategies almost always win out over the complicated models and stock-picking schemes. Don't overcomplicate investing! You'll spend less time worrying and will make more money.

We'll leave putting together an income investing strategy until after we've talked about two other investments, MLPs and REITs.

Dividend Aristocrats

Easily the most popular group of dividend stocks is the Dividend Aristocrats. These are U.S. companies that have increased their dividend every year for at least 25 years.

Companies that have consistently increased their dividend payment have not only outperformed the general market, but they often do so with less risk as well. Increasing your dividend payment over such a long period, even during recessions, shows a strong commitment to returning cash to shareholders.

There are currently 58 companies in the Dividend Aristocrats list. To March 2014, the S&P 500 Dividend Aristocrats posted an annual return of 10.3% over the last ten years compared to a return of 7.4% for all the companies in the S&P 500 over the same period.

Investors like following the Dividend Aristocrats list because it gives them exposure to companies across many different industries. Other groups below may be confined to specific sectors and won't give you the kind of diversification you need if you invest exclusively in that group of stocks.

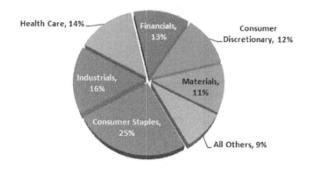

Sector Exposures in Dividend Aristocrats (2015)

Health Care, 14%

Financials, 13%

Consumer Discretionary, 12%

Industrials, 16%

Materials, 11%

Consumer Staples, 25%

All Others, 9%

Utilities

Shares of utility companies are popular with dividend investors because of their consistent payments and low risk business model. Utilities are a special type of company, with a sort of protected status. They trade the ability to increase rates as high as the market will bear for the protection of being one of the few suppliers. This also makes them one of the most predictable returns in the market.

Within the group, investors generally categorize companies by the service provided (electric, water and natural gas) or by whether the company is regulated by a local municipality or not. Each category will mean different risks and rewards. Unregulated providers may be able to raise rates more quickly but will probably not enjoy monopoly protection from competitors. The different service providers may be at risk to prices or shortages for their respective commodity.

One risk to utility companies that you will want to watch out for is increasing interest rates. Since the power of the company to raise rates is often limited, their cash flow and dividends are relatively fixed compared to other stocks. This means that the investment may behave more like a bond than a stock and the share price may fall when interest rates rise. The drop in price should not be too bad and the safety and yield in these companies is still pretty enticing.

Consumer Staples

Companies providing staple goods, or things that are seen as necessity products, are also a common favorite for dividend investors. Like utilities, these companies are typically in very mature industries with stable sales and cash flows. Since sales are so consistent and opportunities for growth are relatively fewer, these companies can afford to pay out more cash as dividends.

Consumer staples may also be referred to as consumer non-cyclical because their products are not generally prone to the rise and fall of the business cycle. Within the group, you find industries like: Beverages (both alcoholic and non-alcoholic), food processors, personal & household products, and tobacco. While you may not agree that alcohol or tobacco products are necessities, people that buy the products generally buy a consistent amount through good times and bad.

XLP Consumer Staples Select Sector SPDR NYSE   ® StockCharts.com
16-Oct-2015   **Op** 49.20 **Hi** 49.68 **Lo** 49.19 **Cl** 49.63 **Vol** 6.9M **Chg** +0.47 (+0.96%) ▲

Not only do they provide strong dividends but consumer staples have easily beaten the return on the overall market over the last decade.

A New Breed of Technology Dividend-Payers

Just twenty years ago, no one would expect a technology company to pay a dividend on its common shares. The tech bubble was just inflating and companies like Oracle (ORCL) and Intel (INTC) needed every penny to pay for their tremendous growth.

Slowing opportunities in growth projects and a huge stockpile of cash has driven some of the bellwether technology names to issue dividends over the last few years. Microsoft (MSFT) started paying out cash in 2003 and Intel offers a yield stronger than many of the consumer staple companies. While growth might have slowed for these companies in developed markets, they still might book strong sales growth in emerging markets and drive higher stock prices as well as a good dividend return.

Of course, dividend payments are still the exception rather than the norm among tech companies. Of the approximate 1,800 technology companies listed on the U.S. exchanges, only 219 pay a dividend and only 105 offer a yield of 2% or higher. The addition of dividends means a strong complement to shareholder returns and a great way to diversify your portfolio from the traditional dividend-paying sectors.

A Dividend Group to Avoid – Highest Yields

Some stocks pay dividend yields so high that it seems like a no-brainer. Unfortunately, like that notorious offer you *can't* refuse, you are better avoiding some of these stocks. There are two issues you need to be aware of when searching for high-yield dividend stocks.

First, is the high dividend yield simply a function of poor price performance? If the shares pay an annual $0.25 per share dividend and have a price of $15 per share, the dividend yield is just under two percent. Now if the price of the shares plummets to just $2.50 per share, the dividend yield vaults to 10%. Of the 181 stocks trading on the NYSE with dividend yields over 8%, nearly half (81) have seen their stock price fall by more than 8% over the past year with the top ten posting losses of more than 20%. A dramatic price drop is usually a sign of tough times for a company and the dividend may have to be cut to protect the business.

Another reason you need to be cautious of high-yielding stocks is that many of these companies keep little back for growth. They pay out nearly all their cash as dividends and must constantly raise money for new projects. Dividend payments from these stocks are usually more inconsistent with very high payments in some quarters and low payments in others. That high yield you think you are getting may not be so high in the near future.

How to Pick Dividend Stocks

There are just as many ways to pick dividend stocks as there are stocks themselves and an entire book could be written on the subject. I've seen every stock screen and every strategy with some as simple as looking for cheap value and others as complex as large computer programs.

As with investing in general, the best strategy is the simplest. Understanding the general business in which a company operates and knowing a few metrics is really all you need to pick good, long-term dividend investments.

Fundamental Analysis

Fundamental analysis refers to looking at the financial data provided by the company to assess its strength relative to competitors and its prospects for future growth. As with any kind of stock analysis, there are a million and one data points to look at but a few basic ideas are all you need to pick good companies that can provide a steady income and price returns to your portfolio.

Let's get some of the most common vocabulary out of the way before talking about how to look at company fundamentals.

Margins are an important metric to follow and measure the profitability of a business. The three margins from the company's income statement are:

- **Gross margin** is the percentage of sales left over after paying for the cost of materials.

- **Operating margin** is the percentage of income left over after all operating expenses have been taken out of sales. This is one of my favorite fundamental metrics because it shows how well management operates the business, growing sales while keeping operating costs under control.

- **Net margin** is the percentage of income left after taking out all income statement items from sales.

When you're looking at the margins of a company, it's helpful to look at the company's history as well as at competitors' margins.

- Is the company becoming more profitable by increasing its margins over the last few years?

- Is the company more or less profitable compared to its competition?

Dividend yield is obviously extremely important for a dividend portfolio and is just the annual dividend per share divided by the stock price. It's what percentage you'll earn over the next year in dividends if the payment doesn't change.

Since the general market offers a yield of around 2%, I like to see yields above 2.5% for my dividend stocks to show management's commitment to returning cash to shareholders.

The **payout ratio** is another important dividend metric. It's the total dividend amount paid divided by the company's earnings. How much of profits is the company paying to shareholders and how much is it keeping back for future growth?

I also like to see a payout ratio of 65% or less when I look for dividend stocks. If a company is paying out more than 65% of its income as dividends, it may not be keeping enough back to grow the company. It may also have a hard time supporting the dividend payment if earnings fall.

Of course, this rule does not apply to REITs or MLPs since they must return more than 90% of their profits to shareholders to keep their tax-advantaged status.

Valuing stocks seems like it should be one of the simplest and most intuitive concepts in investing. Buy low and sell high is the simple mantra. It is rarely as simple as that and there are many different models by which to measure a stocks fair value and its value relative to peers.

The first, and probably the most commonly used metrics are **price multiples**. These are simply the share price divided by another per share amount. Common measures are by earnings, sales, cash flow or book value.

The **price-to-earnings ratio** (P/E) is the most common of the group. Its popularity makes sense because earnings are supposed to measure the profit to owners of the company so the ratio measures how much investors are willing to pay for a share of those profits.

There are two important uses for price-multiples like the P/E ratio. You can compare the ratio with that of competitors. You can also compare a company's current ratio with its historic average.

- Is the company more or less expensive compared to competitors?

- Is the current price multiple more or less expensive compared to the average of the company's multiple over the last few years?

The most important thing to remember about price multiples is that it's a relative measure and cannot tell you the real value of the stock. It measures the stock's price against itself or another stock using the same measurement.

Price multiples will not tell you what the fair value of a company is or how much you should pay for the shares. The fact that a company's shares trade for 15 times its earnings may mean that it is relatively cheaper than a stock trading at 20 times earnings but that does not necessarily mean it's a good buy. The stocks in the sector or even the whole market may be overvalued so buying the cheapest ones may still be paying too much.

Comparing a stock's P/E ratio with its own average over a longer period may help decide whether it is over- or under-valued but you'll need to use other methods to determine fair value.

Many dividend investors prefer a **dividend yield method** of valuation. Since income is the focus of the portfolio, it stands to reason that it should be used as a decisive point whether to buy a stock or not. The idea makes intuitive sense as well. The dividend yield is the current payout divided by the share price so if a stock's share price has outgrown its value then the yield would be relatively low and may not make your cutoff.

For individual stocks, look at the dividend yield over time. If the stock price has increased quickly without the dividend increasing as well, then a very low dividend yield may not be worth your investment.

When you're comparing the dividend yield across different companies, do it only against other stocks in the same sector. If you only invest in stocks with the highest dividend yields, you could end up with all your investments in a couple of sectors like utilities and consumer goods. That means you'll be at risk if something happens to that sector and won't benefit if other sectors do well.

REITs: The Hassle-free Way to Invest in Real Estate

Investing in real estate investment trusts (REITs) is a great way to get real estate exposure for your portfolio without the high cost and management headache of direct ownership in rental houses. The companies remove a lot of the barriers that investors face with other forms of real estate investing.

- **Low start-up cost** – Direct investment in real estate means tens of thousands of dollars or more for a down payment. Shares of REITs can be bought like regular stocks for less than one hundred dollars.

- **Diversification** – It's extremely difficult for most investors to buy enough properties, differentiated by location and type, to get safety through diversification. REITs hold hundreds of properties from all over the country or even the world.

- **Management** – Hiring someone to manage a few properties is extremely expensive and you may not have the time to manage your own properties. REITs are managed by experts in real estate with efficiency through hundreds or thousands of properties.

The biggest advantage to REITs is their tax advantages. REITs are structured under a special law that protects them from corporate taxes. If they pay out at least 90% of their annual income to shareholders, they don't have to pay taxes as do other companies. That means an extremely efficient way to manage real estate and more money in your pocket as a shareholder. The tax advantage is so powerful that regular companies like

McDonald's and Sears have considered selling their locations into a REIT and then renting the space.

There are primarily two types of REITs, an equity-type and a mortgage-type. Equity REITs own and operate real estate. Mortgage REITs lend money for the purchase of real estate and make money off the interest on the loans. Equity REITs are 90% of the stocks traded and a better investment for income so we'll spend the rest of the time focusing on the segment.

Because of the advantages of REITs and the popularity of real estate as an investment, shares of REITs are widely held by pension funds, insurance companies, bank portfolios and by individual investors.

With the exception of the recent housing bubble, real estate has historically been an extremely stable investment. Commercial property benefits from the stability of long-term leases and property value that rises by at least the rate of inflation.

According to the National Association of REITs (NAREIT), over the four decades to 2013, REIT investors earned an average 8.0% each year in dividends and 5.5% from share price increase.

For reference, that 13.5% total return is nearly twice the 7.2% annual return on stocks in the S&P 500 over the same period.

Just like investing in stocks of traditional companies, you can buy shares of individual REIT companies or shares of funds that hold REITs. Even though many REITs offer diversification through properties of varying location and property-type, funds offer one more layer of diversification.

Investing in REITs

Investing in REITs can provide a great stream of income as well as the potential for long-term returns. Since most REITs hold specific types of commercial properties, you'll want to make sure you diversify your portfolio by buying REITs across different property types; i.e. industrial, retail, multi-family and office.

Understand that REITs are different than other companies so they are not valued the same. Since depreciation is a very important part of a real estate business, but is removed from income, the earnings per share (EPS) reported by REITs is not a valid measure of income. Instead of EPS, investors look at the company's Funds from Operations (FFO) or adjusted FFO. The FFO is a more accurate measure of how the REIT is generating cash for shareholders.

The table shows a basic calculation for FFO and adjusted FFO. While it can be overwhelming for new investors, it's intuitive if you think about it. A REIT's true operational performance is the money it makes including the benefit from depreciation but not including one-time things like selling its own properties.

A word of warning, you'll see the calculation for FFO stay pretty consistent but companies and analysts differ on how to calculate adjusted FFO. When you're comparing different companies, just make sure all the calculations methods are the same.

How to Calculate Funds from Operations (FFO) for a REIT

	Net Income
Plus	Depreciation and Amortization from Real Estate
Minus	Interest Income
Minue	Gains or (plus Losses) on Sale of Real Estate

Equals	**Funds from Operations**

Minus	Capital Spending for Maintenance
Minus	Straight-line Rent over Contract
Minus	Non-cash unrealized Gains

Equals	**Adjusted FFO**

Once you've got a REIT's FFO or AFFO, you can use it to value the company much like earnings are used for other companies. Dividing the price by FFO will tell you how "expensive" the shares are compared to other REITs. You can also compare the REIT's growth in FFO over the years to make sure they are progressively growing funds.

Analyzing individual REITs can get just as complicated as with other stocks. If you are going to analyze and invest in individual companies, I would suggest putting some money in exchange traded funds like the Vanguard REIT ETF (VNQ) which itself holds REIT stocks. That will help diversify your investments while still giving you the chance for higher returns on your own analysis.

Risks in Real Estate REIT Investing

There are two primary risks with REIT investing, interest rates and property cycles. Both of these are not a problem for long-term investors who will see their investments grow and return cash over decades.

Since REITs pay out most of their cash to shareholders every year, they constantly have to take out loans for growth and operations. Rising interest rates means higher interest expense that might eat into the amount of cash the company can return to shareholders. This effect is partially offset by a strengthening economy, usually happening at the same time as interest rate increases, which means stronger rental payments on real estate.

While real estate prices generally go up over time, it's not always a steady upward climb. Prices for commercial real estate, the majority of REIT holdings, are going to rise and fall with the business cycle and the prospect for rent. This means being able to hold your REIT investments without panicking during a recession.

MLPs: Strike Oil or Make Money off Those Who Do

As we saw with real estate investment trusts (REITs), the government has allowed tax advantages on certain types of investments. As difficult as it is to "beat" the market and earn a respectable rate of return on a portfolio, these tax breaks make for opportunities that you just cannot pass up.

Anytime a company can avoid corporate taxes while managing a certain type of investment or anytime you can avoid income taxes on your investments, returns should naturally be higher compared to the taxed alternative.

Master Limited Partnerships (MLPs) are another type of tax-advantaged investment structure that actually benefits from avoidance of corporate taxes and personal income taxes. It's a combination you do not want to ignore.

What are Master Limited Partnerships?

MLPs are a special business structure that combines the benefits of a corporation with the tax advantages of a partnership. Since 1981, the U.S. Congress has allowed these businesses to avoid paying corporate income taxes if 90% or more of their income was passed through to the partners.

In 1987, Congress restricted MLPs to those companies in the energy, real estate or finance sectors. Most real estate firms have opted to go with the REIT structure, which is similar. As of December 2013, most (84%) of MLPs were in the energy sector.

Further, most energy MLPs (80%) are in the midstream segment of the sector.

- Energy companies in the upstream segment are involved in exploration and drilling for oil & natural gas. They are "upstream" or removed furthest from the retail energy customers.

- Energy companies in the midstream segment are involved in transportation and storage of energy through pipelines and storage facilities.

- Energy companies in the downstream segment are involved in refining, i.e. turning oil into usable products like gasoline, and selling products to customers.

Midstream energy companies own pipeline and storage facilities and typically get paid for volume of oil or gas that they transport. This is an important point because it removes some of the risk around oil & gas prices. Midstream MLPs may do well even when energy prices are falling because they are paid on the amount of energy demanded rather than the price.

As a result of the tax benefits to the MLP structure, many energy companies have sold their pipeline and storage assets to an MLP. The energy company gets cash for the assets and the MLP can manage them more efficiently, without having to pay taxes.

MLPs are generally controlled by a General Partner (GP) and often don't even have employees. The MLP simply is a company structure to own the pipelines and storage facilities while the GP manages them by contracting with companies for transportation and storage. The GP takes a fee for management and sometimes an incentive percentage of profits.

In addition to the corporate tax benefits, MLP investors also benefit on their own income taxes. Since MLP investors are partners in the assets, the tax benefits from depreciation are passed directly through along with the earnings.

Remember that with REITs, the company benefits by being able to write off the annual amount of real estate depreciation before it passes earnings on to investors.

MLPs pass these depreciation benefits directly through to investors, which use the depreciation to offset the income they receive from the partnership. As a result, investors generally pay current year taxes only on a small portion (usually 10% to 20%) of the income they receive from the MLP.

The other side to this is that the amount offset by depreciation lowers your cost in the investment. That means you pay higher taxes when you sell the investment. When you sell an MLP investment, a portion of the gain will be taxed as income rather than capital gains.

There is one way around this though...never sell your MLP investments. These are investments in real assets, energy pipelines and storage, which will be around for decades and in constant demand. Best yet, if an MLP investment is passed on through an estate, your heirs will not have to pay the taxes you owed. The cost of the shares is marked up to the point where they inherited the investment and all the taxes owed are wiped out.

One downside to MLP investments is the special tax form you will receive every year, called a schedule K-1 form. This form lists out the income, deductions, losses and credits on the partnership. This helps to calculate how much of your income is taxable after depreciation. Some investors find it difficult, or at least a hassle, to work through the K-1 form.

Any tax accountant should easily be able to handle the forms though they may charge a little extra. Most tax software packages have a relatively easy walk-through to putting your MLP investments on your taxes.

Why invest in MLPs?

The tax advantages of MLPs have helped them outperform other investments in the past. Over nearly two decades since 1996, MLPs have offered a total annual return of about 15% versus 8.6% on stocks and 5.6% on corporate bonds.

For income investors, MLPs offer some of the highest payouts in investing. As of year-end 2013, energy MLPs offered an average yield of 5.5%; compared to 4.4% for REITs, 2% for stocks and 2.5% for bonds. The higher income and deferred tax advantages make MLPs some of the most preferred investments of people living off their investment income.

How to Invest in MLPs

MLP investments trade just like regular stocks and can be bought cheaply through online investing sites like E*Trade or TD Ameritrade. Technically, your investment in an MLP is for "units" of the partnership rather than stock and the income you receive is called "distributions" rather than "dividends." There is really no difference though and only the purists will be annoyed if you call it stocks or dividends.

As with REITs, some of the popular measures for stocks like the price-earnings ratio are not applicable for MLP investments. Instead, MLP investors primarily use two metrics called Distributable Cash Flow (DCF) and the Coverage Ratio.

Distributable cash flow measures the partnership's ability to generate cash after expenses and costs to maintain the business. Since MLPs return most of their annual cash to investors, it is a measure of how much is available to shareholders.

Calculating DCF is straight-forward and just involves adding back non-cash items like depreciation back to net income. These items are removed from net income on the company's income statement for tax reporting purposes but do not represent an actual outflow of cash.

Maintenance capital expenditures are the annual amount spent to keep all the pipelines or storage facilities operating normally. Removing this amount leaves you with how much cash the company could distribute without having to worry about infrastructure wearing out and losing business. Most partnerships will calculate DCF for you in their financial statements.

The coverage ratio is another important measure. While partnerships could distribute all their DCF, it is safer to retain some cash for future growth or spending. The coverage ratio is the DCF divided by the amount the partnership actually distributed over the last year.

Coverage Ratio = DCF / Cash Distributed to Investors

When analyzing different MLP investments, you want to make sure the distributable cash flow is increasing at a fairly steady rate. This means the partnership is doing a good job of generating more cash to return to investors. You also want to make sure the distribution payment is not at risk by looking at the coverage ratio. There's no rule but I like to make sure the company has a coverage ratio of at least 1.2 times (DCF divided by distributed cash = 1.2 or higher).

Looking at different MLP investments, you will also want to pay attention to how much the General Partner benefits from its management. Besides a fee, usually around 2%, many general partners get special payouts called Incentive Distribution Rights (IDRs).

These IDRs give the general partner the right to an increasing percentage of the cash flow depending on the distribution per unit. It favors the general partner over investors and many investor groups have fought against the practice. Some MLPs have started to manage their own assets or pay the general partner a fixed-amount instead of a percentage.

Long-term investors do not generally have to worry too much about picking the perfect MLP investment. Invest equally across a group of five different MLPs with relatively stable increases in DCF and good coverage ratios. This will help smooth out your total investment returns even if one MLP stumbles. Do not sell out of your MLP investments. Hold your MLP investments forever and enjoy the tax benefit.

Since MLPs are almost exclusively energy companies, keep an eye on your total exposure to stocks and bonds of energy companies. Holding 10% of your portfolio in MLPs may not seem like you are exposed to weakness in energy prices but factoring in your 10% holding of energy stocks like Exxon Mobil and another 5% holding of bonds from energy companies presents a different picture.

While there are exchange traded funds (ETFs) that hold MLP company shares, I do not generally recommend them. Investment in MLP funds will avoid getting the K-1 form every year for your taxes but the funds do not enjoy the same tax benefits.

Regulatory requirements mean that most MLP exchange traded funds have to register as regular corporations, meaning they pay corporate taxes on their profits. Losing out on the tax advantage means that MLP funds underperform direct investing in individual MLPs every year. On your side, you will pay regular income taxes on the full amount of income you receive from the fund.

Risks and Return on MLP Investments

As with any sector, MLP companies are prone to overbuilding of pipelines and other assets to later face overcapacity later on. The boom in U.S. energy production has meant that demand for transportation of oil and gas has kept up with building so we haven't seen any problems but it's always a possibility.

While MLPs generally get paid on the volume of energy they transport or store, they still carry some risk on lower energy prices. There are a couple of reasons for this, besides the fact that some revenue is tied to the price of oil or gas. Falling energy prices may weaken investor sentiment for all types of energy investments including MLPs. Uncertainty in the energy sector due to falling prices make it more difficult for MLPs to secure funding and contracts for services.

MLP investments carry some interest rate risk, similar to what we saw in REIT investments. Because the companies pay out almost all income each year, they must continually find new funding by issuing bonds or selling stock units. If interest rates go up, it becomes more expensive to issue debt and interest expense will increase. If interest rates keep rising, the partnership may issue more unit shares instead of debt, which dilutes your investment.

Most of the risks to MLP investing are short-term cyclical risks, not really of much importance to a long-term investor. Economic cycles are bound to come and go, taking interest rates and energy prices higher and lower.

Long-term income investors should not worry about these risks and can be confident that MLP investments will provide strong returns over a decade or longer.

Since MLPs are already tax-advantaged, they are not appropriate investments for your 401k, IRA or other retirement accounts. Tax-exempt investors and some retirement plans may be subject to unrelated business taxable income (UBTI) on MLP investments so do not hold these investments in your retirement accounts.

The revolution in U.S. energy production is a generational phenomenon and should mean increasing or stable demand for oil & gas transportation for a very long time. The tax advantages of MLP investments should drive a respectable return, if not one that is higher than traditional stocks and bonds.

Even on a conservative estimate, you should be able to earn an income return of between 3% and 5% each year from MLPs and a similar return on the investment value. A total annual return of 6% to 10% or higher is very attractive, especially when you consider that much of your income return will not be taxed until much later.

A Step-by-Step Dividend Investing Strategy

We'll use what we've learned in previous chapters to create a step-by-step strategy not only for building a portfolio of income-producing stocks but for your whole portfolio.

Through the strategy, we'll look at the right amounts of dividend stocks, MLPs and REITs to have in your portfolio according to your investment needs.

We'll wrap it up with how to juice your dividend income with reinvestment plans, how to maintain your portfolio and how to know when it's time to sell.

Why most investors lose money

Despite all the analysis of investments on TV and across the internet, investing really isn't about stocks and companies – it's about YOU!

The stock market and other investments are going to provide a return for a certain amount of risk. The only question you need to be asking is how much risk will you take for how much return?

Most people miss this point and just invest haphazardly across a bunch of stocks. They end up getting beaten and bruised by the market because their investments aren't customized to their needs.

That's why the first step in any investing strategy is to create a personal investment plan. This written plan is going to look at how much you need for your specific goals and how much risk you want to take. It's only by knowing these two key elements that you'll be able to pick the right investments for you.

Step 1: Creating your personal investment plan

A personal investment plan is one of the most important concepts in personal finance. Unfortunately, it's also one of the most neglected. Instead of taking the time to figure out what people really need to reach their financial goals, it's far easier to just throw recommendations at them and create a frenzy for stocks.

That's why the average investor return was just 2.6% annually for the decade to 2013, even as the stock market returned 7.4% and the bond market offered a 4.6% annual return over the period.

Investors don't know where they're going so they trade in and out of stocks, hoping to magically appear at their financial destination in retirement.

A personal investment plan is your roadmap to meeting your financial goals.

That roadmap starts with finding your destination. Estimate how much you'll need in retirement and for different financial goals. Be sure to include any large expenses like education and financial gifts. The general rule is that you'll need 80% of your current income in retirement. This estimate may not work for everyone but it's a good place to start.

You'll also need to look over your budget and decide how much you can save towards your financial goals each year. Your monthly savings might rise and fall slightly but you just want a rough estimate of how much you can save.

Finding the annual return you'll need to meet your financial goals is pretty easy through retirement calculators.

For example, if you need $1,000,000 when you retire in 29 years and have $180,000 saved and can save another $5,500 annually then your return needed would be just 4.5% annually.

A lot of people don't realize how moderate of a return they actually need so they load up on risky stocks, hoping for double-digit gains every year. They end up taking too much risk and panic-selling when the market crashes.

The final piece of your personal investment plan is finding the level of risk you're comfortable with taking in investments. Your risk level depends on two factors, your ability to take risk and your willingness.

Ability to take risks depends on how much money you have and how long you've got to when you'll be depending on your investments for living expenses. If you've already got a very large nest egg relative to how much you need, you might be able to take more risk. Conversely, if you are approaching retirement and are not yet to your financial goal then you do not want to see your investments wiped out in a market crash.

Willingness to take risks is much more an emotional preference. Are you comfortable with big changes in your wealth or would you rather a slow and steady approach? Are you a gambler or someone that prefers the insured and certain path?

There are Risk Tolerance questionnaires available on the internet. I've put together a simple test below to help you find your own tolerance for risk.

Each question is associated with a point scale. Give yourself one point for the first answer, two points for the second, and so on.

1) When do you expect to be using the money from your investments?

- Less than a year

- 1-3 years

- 3-10 years

- After more than 10 years

If you are going to need your money in less than a few years, your investment risk tolerance is going to be very low. You cannot afford for the stock market to take a nose dive and wait for the recovery. If you won't need the money for decades, you can accept the stock market ups and downs that come every 3-5 years. *(Score from one to four points)*

2) How important is it that you reach this particular financial goal?

- Couldn't live without it

- I'll get by but it will be difficult

- No significant change in lifestyle but I will be disappointed

The importance of reaching a particular financial goal is something most don't think about with their investments. They lump investments for retirement and education in with their vacation money and everything else. You will be able to tolerate a little more risk, and potentially see higher returns, with less important financial goals. *(Score from one to three points)*

3) How long will you be spending money from the investment?

- I will spend it all immediately

- It will probably be spent between a year and five years

- I will be spending the money down over a long-term, greater than 10 years

If you are going to be needing all or most of the money at a specific date, or over a short period, then you will have less tolerance for risk. Tuition expenses won't wait a few years for the market to recover. On the other hand, if you can withdraw money gradually and let the rest accumulate, you may be able to handle a little more risk. *(Score from one to three points)*

4) How often do you sell your investments after buying them?

- Usually within one or two years

- After three to five years

- I hold on to investments for a very long time, greater than eight or ten years

Notice there is no choice for less than a year, that's not investing but gambling on the short-term craziness of the market. Active investors, those buying and selling more frequently, are usually able to handle a little more risk in their investments without losing much sleep. *(Score from one to three points)*

5) If a stock I owned lost 30% of its value over the course of a few months, as happened broadly in 2008, I would most likely...

- Sell all of the investment

- Sell a portion of the investment

- Sell nothing but do nothing

- Buy more of the investment

Be honest here. If you absolutely cringe at the idea of losing money in your portfolio, even if it is in just one stock, then your investment risk tolerance is low. There is nothing wrong with wanting the safe and steady. *(Score from one to four points)*

6) When the stock market is declining rapidly, I generally sell some of my investments to protect my money

- Yes, I sell a lot and feel better doing so

- I may sell some but am disappointed

- Really can't tell what I would do

- No, I wouldn't sell anything but I may be a little anxious

- No, I buy more all the way down and wait for the recovery

This is related to the previous question but a little more general. Think carefully about how you would feel, maybe using the past financial crisis as a guide. If you can really get by and not worry about your investments losing money for a period of several years, then you are able to tolerate more risk. *(Score from one to five points)*

7) The chart below shows three portfolios with different risk and potential returns. Choose the one with which you would be most comfortable. For example, portfolio A may earn $593 but may lose $164 while portfolio C may earn much more but may also lose much more.

This question is pretty straight-forward. If you would feel comfortable risking the loss of nearly $4,000 for the chance to gain $5,000 then you are clearly able to tolerate more investment risk. If you would rather only risk a much smaller amount, then you are less risk tolerant. *(Score from one to three points)*

8) What kind of stocks do you generally prefer?

- High-growth companies making tech advances that could jump quickly

- Established companies with some potential for growth

- Mature companies that may not be headline news but pay stable dividends

This isn't meant to help you pick stocks but to get a feel for the kind of investment in which you are comfortable. Shares of companies like Coca-Cola are not going to make you a millionaire overnight but the odds of losses are very low. Shares of that hot tech-startup could surge with a patent discovery but the company could also go bust, losing all your money. In which would you be comfortable putting your money? *(Score from one to three points)*

9) What type of bonds do you generally prefer?

- High-yield bonds that offer high interest rates even if the company is less secure

- Tax-free bonds paying lower rates but backed by governments and cities

Even fixed-income bonds can be risky and attract a certain type of investor. Would you prefer the slow and steady of government-backed bonds, even if they don't pay much, or do you need a little more risk even in your bond investments? *(Score from one to two points)*

10) My current and future income sources are...

- Uncertain, I work independently and income varies

- The industry in which I work is cyclical and layoffs are common

- Nothing is certain but I have good seniority and should not have to worry

- I have contracts in place that will nearly guarantee my employment or a strong severance

You need to balance you financial risk with your investment risk. Many that work in the financial markets, i.e. stock traders and advisors, have very little risk tolerance because their income is directly tied to the markets. A market collapse or recession may severely limit their income so they do not want to simultaneously suffer investment losses as well. On the other hand, tenured professors and others with contracted employment may be able to take a little more investment risk since their income is all but guaranteed. *(Score from one to four points)*

While it's not an exact measure, the questions above should be able to pinpoint your risk tolerance pretty closely. There are a total of 10 to 34 points available.

Score < 14 points

You do not want much risk at all in your investments and should stick with mostly bonds and other safe investments.

Score between 15 and 19 points

You have a low tolerance for risk and will still want most of your investments in bonds but can put a little more towards stocks and real estate.

Score between 20 and 24 points

You have a medium tolerance for risk and should be ok with about equal investments in stocks and bonds

Score above 25 points

You have a fairly high tolerance for risk and can put more investments to stocks compared to safer investments.

Use the annual return you need and your risk tolerance to decide how much of your total portfolio you need in different asset classes.

There are five general asset classes – stocks, bonds, real estate, commodities and alternative investments. Each asset class is comprised of investments that share common growth drivers and is different from the other assets. There will be some overlap between assets, for example real estate and commodities both react similarly to inflation but they are clearly different in most respects.

Within each asset class, investments are further separated into groups that share similarities. Within bonds, you can invest in foreign or domestic issues, debt specific to an industry or different types of debt. Commodities can be agricultural, precious metals or metals used in industrial production.

The asset classes are important for a couple of reasons:

- Different assets offer different returns for different levels of risk. I've included a comparison chart of risk and returns below. If you have a low tolerance for risk and do not need a high return to meet your financial goals, you'll want to invest mostly in assets on the left-side of the chart.

- Investing in different asset classes helps to diversify your risks. Some investments will rise while others are not doing so well. This will help to smooth out your returns instead of turning your portfolio into a stress-inducing roller coaster.

The Risk – Return Tradeoff

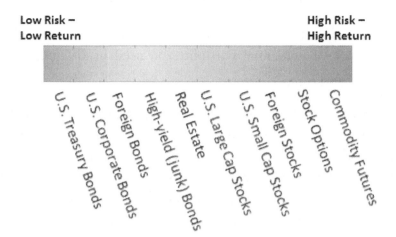

Low Risk –
Low Return

High Risk –
High Return

U.S. Treasury Bonds
U.S. Corporate Bonds
Foreign Bonds
High-yield (junk) Bonds
Real Estate
U.S. Large Cap Stocks
U.S. Small Cap Stocks
Foreign Stocks
Stock Options
Commodity Futures

Diversification is the key to any investment strategy. The idea of diversification is that not all investments will react similarly to changes in the economic environment or sentiment for stocks. By combining different investments within a portfolio, you can smooth out your returns even over the worst of times.

Of course, there is a price to pay for lower risk in your portfolio. If you were to invest in only one stock and it soared three-fold, your returns would be amazing. If you spread your investments over ten stocks, your averaged returns across the portfolio would be less spectacular. The price of averaged returns is well worth it because the value of your portfolio won't be at risk of catastrophic loss if any one stock stumbles.

Most investors really only need a mix of stocks, bonds and real estate to meet their financial goals. Investing in commodities and stock options opens your portfolio up to more risk and overcomplicates your strategy.

How much you invest in each asset class is going to change as you get older because your risk tolerance will change. As you get closer to needing the money from your investments, you won't be able to withstand the greater risk in stocks.

Look at this example as a guide for changing your allocation in stocks, bonds and real estate.

Life Stage Investing - Matching Risk with Your Needs

Stocks	70%	60%	50%	30%
Bonds	15%	15%	25%	50%
Real Estate	15%	25%	25%	20%

* Percentages are approximate and may not be appropriate for all investors

Step 2: Creating your Stock Investing Plan

Once you know how much of your money you want to put in stocks, it's time to think about which stocks you should buy.

We carry the idea of diversification into stocks as well. The stock market is separated into nine different sectors of companies.

The Nine Stock Sectors

Getting your diversification in stocks means investing in each of the major sectors. Try to pick a mix of large companies and small companies.

Financials	Energy	Healthcare
Technology	Materials	Consumer Staples
Utilities	Industrials	Consumer Discretionary

Companies in each sector serve or produce a common product category. The sectors are further separated into hundreds of industries which all focus more closely on a common product or service.

You will want to invest in a mix of stocks from all the sectors but may want to invest more in specific sectors depending on your risk tolerance.

Stocks within utilities, healthcare, and consumer staples tend to be less risky than other sectors. Stocks within technology, consumer discretionary and financials may be more risky but may also provide higher returns.

When deciding how much of each stock to buy, I would generally start with around 2% or 3% of the total amount you want to invest. That means even a total loss in one stock will not be catastrophic to your portfolio. It also means that a stock has to nearly double before it gets to be too large a percentage of your portfolio and you need to sell.

When looking for individual companies to add to my dividend portfolio, I like to look for stocks within one of the three themes. Each theme serves a special purpose and helps to focus my portfolio to my own goals and investing needs.

Utilities and Consumer Staples for Yield and Safety

One of the first things investors look for in dividend-paying companies is a consistent income and safety from the ups and downs of the regular market cycle. Even if dividend stocks did not consistently outperform their non-dividend peers, you will love the protection they provide when your neighbor is tearing his hair out because his momentum stocks tumbled.

Few sectors provide the safety and yield of utilities and consumer staples. In mature or semi-regulated industries, these companies have non-cyclical cash flow that increases at a steady rate in the worst of times as well as the best.

Stocks in the utilities sector offer one of the highest dividend yields as a group, around 3.6% for the Select Sector SPDR Utilities Fund (XLU). The sector can be further separated into regulated and unregulated services or through their different segments like water, gas, electric or alternative energy. Even the unregulated companies operate in a relatively limited competitive environment with allowable rate increases and steady profits.

Companies in the consumer staples sector may not pay a yield as high as those in the utilities sector but growth is usually slightly higher. The group pays an average yield of 2.5% but still finds growth opportunities in emerging markets and share prices should add to total returns. The companies sell products that everyone needs in their daily lives and have built immense brand loyalty over decades. There is relatively little threat of new competitors coming into the space because of the huge economies of scale the companies have built through global production and distribution.

Investing in utilities and consumer staples is not without risk. For the safety of stable growth, you often give up some return so do not expect the share prices to shoot higher in any given year. Since utilities cannot increase their rates quickly, their shares react like bonds when interest rates rise. That means when interest rates increase, other investments may be more attractive and the shares lose their value. Companies of consumer staples are able to increase their prices a little faster but competition usually limits the ability and neither sector is a good hedge against inflation.

New Breed for Growth

For portfolio growth, the new breed of technology companies that pay dividends are a great addition. These companies still see relatively strong sales growth in developed markets and faster growth opportunities in emerging markets around the world. Often, these companies also buy growth through acquisitions of new technologies or patents.

Many of the new breed of tech dividend-payers do not generally pay a high yield so you will need to sacrifice some current income for growth. Companies in the sector face more competition than in sectors like utilities or consumer staples so there is no guarantee of higher share prices. I like to focus on an established management team that has historically proven it can execute on competitive goals and keep the company relevant.

Real Asset Structures for Inflation Protection

The companies that own hard assets like pipeline MLPs and REITs are a good addition for inflation protection, though they can pay off in other ways as well. While commercial property and energy infrastructure may need maintenance from time to time, these assets generally tend to increase in value with the decline in dollar purchasing power. Their productive capacity is the same; the only thing that is different is the value of the dollar so the assets cost more.

Another benefit of the group is the tax-advantages gained by either investors or the companies themselves. Companies in MLPs and REITs avoid corporate income taxes so it is a much more financially-efficient way to operate the assets that at a traditional company. This means higher profits than would normally be earned. On an individual basis, some of the dividends (called distributions in this case) may be tax-deferred as a return of capital.

Within MLPs specifically, the new energy revolution in the United States is driving the need for more pipeline transportation and storage. Since most of these companies book their revenue on volume rather than commodity prices, they can still see strong cash flows even when oil prices fall.

The real estate bubble and subsequent bust may actually benefit investors in real estate going forward. The commercial and residential real estate markets got crushed during the bust and many regions are still seeing strong price gains back to fair value. The memory of the bubble should keep markets from overheating for a long time and property prices could continue their historically stable climb higher.

The risk to MLPs and REITs is that they may someday lose their tax-advantaged status. This is unlikely but the loss of tax benefits and the resulting hit to investor sentiment could send the shares down sharply. The lost tax revenue is not a lot for the government and the groups have powerful lobbying to make sure they continue to save on taxes.

Since my own investing needs are fairly conservative, aiming for about a 5% annual return with minimal risk, I hold much more of my dividend portfolio in safety stocks like utilities and consumer stables along with some MLPs and REITs. I don't completely neglect dividend growth stocks but do not have much money invested in the group.

These three themes are not the only ones you'll want to check out for your stock portfolio. I highlight opportunities in emerging market stocks in the fourth book of the Step-by-Step Investing series. Cultural preferences and even government regulations mean that a lot of emerging market companies offer very attractive dividends and economic growth in the country can provide for price gains as well.

Step 3: Growing your Dividend Investments

A dividend reinvestment plan (DRIP) is an offer by a company or brokerage account that allows you to automatically buy additional shares with your dividend payments. Rather than cash deposited in your account on the payment date, you will receive new shares in the stock.

There are really two advantages of DRIPs. First, there are usually little or no fees to reinvesting your dividends. Depending on how much you normally pay to buy shares, this could be a big discount over time. Most programs allow you to buy fractional shares as well so you do not have to wait for your dividends to be reinvested in a whole share.

The biggest advantage of DRIPs is the effect of compounding returns over time. Each share or fractional share that you buy with your dividends is a larger ownership in the company and means more dividends in the future.

Reinvesting your dividends can make a huge difference in your portfolio. Reinvesting the meager dividend payment on a small portfolio today may not seem like it would amount to much but it adds up.

If you had invested $10,000 in Coca-Cola shares in 1964, the difference between reinvesting or not is more than one million dollars!

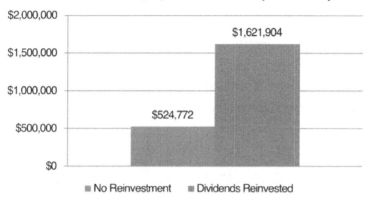

Portfolio Value of $10,000 in Coca-Cola (1964 - 2014)

No Reinvestment — Dividends Reinvested

Potential disadvantages of DRIPs

Dividend reinvestment is not without its disadvantages. You are essentially putting more of your eggs in one basket with a constant reinvestment into the same company. This could set you up for big losses on your portfolio if that company ever falls on hard times.

Reinvestment plans can be stopped at any time so the disadvantages may not be as permanent as they appear. Many plans even allow you to only reinvest a portion of the dividends instead of the full amount.

Setting up your dividend reinvestment plan

Whether you have all of your investments in one particular brokerage account or with individual companies, setting up a dividend reinvestment plan is usually straight forward and simple. For your investments held in a brokerage account, call the customer service line and ask which shares offer DRIPs or if you can enroll your entire account at once. Even if a particular company does not offer a DRIP, your brokerage may offer the service.

You can also go directly to a company's website to see if they offer a DRIP for shares. Contact the company's Investor Relations or Shareholder Services department. They will be able to tell you how to enroll for the program as well as any fees or discounts.

Step 4: Maintaining your Investment Portfolio

Making money on your investments can be intoxicating. You'll notice that your portfolio value increased by several thousand dollars on one strong day and you'll be hooked.

This is where investing gets dangerous.

Too many investors actively watch the TV shows, the websites and all the other places for stock market analysis and start thinking they can 'beat' the market. What started out as a plan to beat your own financial goals and a moderate return becomes a game to get the highest return possible.

And that is how people lose money in stocks and never see their portfolio gain to meet their goals.

Unless you are working in investments, providing advice on a daily basis, you don't need to check your investments more than monthly – no quarterly – wait, annually!

But what if you hear a particularly juicy tip about a stock? What if one of the stocks you own just posted a bad quarter of sales?

Resist the temptation because it really doesn't matter.

First, any news you are hearing will be instantly reflected in the stock price. There are countless traders, brokers and hedge funds sitting by their screens all day and are instantly trading on the news. Rushing in to buy or sell shares just means you are late to the game.

Second, there is always information floating around the markets. Stocks will be too expensive to some and a screaming buy to others. Constantly listening to this market noise will have you buying and selling all the time. The only people that profit from that are those collecting the trading fees.

Think of your investment account more like a savings account. Put money in every month. At the end of every three or six months, use the money you've accumulated to buy more shares of the stocks you own or to buy other companies.

Every year, check the value of your stocks and the value of your total investment by sector and asset class. Have stocks soared higher, taking their value to 50% of your portfolio when you were only planning on holding 30% of your wealth in stocks? Has one company's stock jumped or fallen significantly?

Your annual check-up isn't about timing the market but about correcting these imbalances. If the imbalance isn't too great, say you've got 35% in stocks instead of your 30% target, then save your money and don't worry about it.

This kind of rebalancing serves two purposes:

- You never move too far away from your target percentages in assets or in sectors. This helps to keep your risk where you want it.

- You are more likely to be selling the investments that have gone up and may be relatively expensive. You're taking your profits and giving your losers a chance to rebound.

When to sell a dividend stock

There may be rare occasions when you should sell a stock in your portfolio. The reasons are probably fewer than you think and really come down to whether the stock fits with your overall portfolio strategy.

- Has management decided not to support the dividend or other cash return to shareholders?

- Has management made unethical decisions with which you are not comfortable supporting as a shareholder?

- Have the shares done so incredibly well that they are too large a portion of your portfolio?

Only in extreme cases would I make the decision to sell a stock outside of my quarterly or annual review. Since prices immediately reflect any new information, there's nothing to be gained by rushing to your computer to sell.

Unless you are constantly putting money into the same stock, you shouldn't have to worry about it becoming too big a portion of your total investment. Only if a stock surges and is more than 5% or 6% of your total portfolio should you think about selling some off.

The simplicity in this investing strategy is going to be in contrast to the vast majority of 'advice' you'll see on TV or the internet. Take it from someone that has worked in the markets for more than a decade. Nobody 'really' knows where stocks are going and the only people making money off the complicated strategies and advice are those collecting the fees or selling their analysis.

Keep it simple and send me a thank you note in 20 years.

A Special Request

I hope you've enjoyed Step-by-Step Dividend Investing and found the advice to be helpful in putting together your investing strategy. Throughout the book, I've tried to emphasize the benefit to a simple and basic strategy that meets YOUR financial goals. There's no lack of ways to complicate your investing strategy but the simplest approach will get you to where you want to be with the least amount of headache and sleepless nights.

I'd like to ask one favor as you finish reading the book. Reader reviews are extremely important to the success of a book on Amazon. Reviews play a big part in determining the rank of a book and how many people see it when searching.

If you found the book to be helpful, would you please leave a review on the Amazon page?

It's really easy to do and does not have to be a long, detailed review.

Please click here to leave a review on Amazon

- Just go to the book's page on Amazon (or through the link above) and click on "customer reviews" or scroll down and click on "Write a customer review"

- Your review can be as short as a sentence or as long as you like. Just try describing what you liked about the book and any particular points from a chapter.

I always appreciate honest reviews. Thank you so much!

Resources

Round out your investing plan with the best investments in stocks, emerging markets and bonds. Check out the other three books in the Step-by-Step series:

Learn the secret to building an investing strategy that will meet YOUR needs. The first book in the series covers 10 basic rules of investing you must remember to avoid losing money. You'll get the secret to winning the stock market game as well as a step-by-step strategy for buying stocks. *Click here to buy Step-by-Step Investing*.

Learn the secret to bond investing and how to balance your investments with safety. This book covers how to buy bonds and a simple strategy that will provide a stable income stream you can live on. *Click here to buy Step-by-Step Bond Investing*.

Learn how to add growth to your investments through stocks from the fastest growing countries in the world. This book shows you how to boost returns and lower risk by diversifying in emerging markets. *Click here to buy Step-by-Step Emerging Market Investing*.

See through the BS and scams in passive income strategies to start building a real source of income today in blogging, real estate, stocks and bonds.

NO fluff, NO theories, and NO sugar coating – just the detailed process on how I put together an income from four sources and make money whether I work or not. *Click here to buy The Passive Income Myth.*

News and Professional Organizations

Check out these websites for news and detailed data on the income investments covered in this book.

National Association of Publicly Traded Partnerships (NAPTP) – trade organization for MLP investments with news and information

National Association of Real Estate Investment Trusts (NAREIT) – Information, news and research on REITs and Real Estate

Yahoo Finance – An excellent resource for stock information including charts, data and headlines.

Bloomberg – Business and finance news resource that keeps it objective. You'll see some analyst commentary but the ideas are usually fairly balanced.

Morningstar – Professional source of data and company financial information. There is a lot of analysis and advice on the site. Most of it is objective and helpful but avoid using it to make short-term investment decisions.

Investing and Personal Finance Blogs

Check out these blogs for more advice on personal finance and meeting your long-term goals. Blogs here were chosen for their rational and measured perspective, favoring a long-term approach instead of get-rich-quick schemes.

PeerFinance101 – My blog on personal finance and achieving financial freedom. Financial freedom isn't about getting rich but getting the life you want and making money decisions around that goal. Share your own stories of financial success or learn from others stories.

Side Hustle Nation – A community of part-time entrepreneurs earning financial independence through small business. It's a great resource for finding your passion and turning your hobby into a money-maker.

Barbara Friedberg Personal Finance – Barbara worked as an investment portfolio manager before launching her blog, offering advice following many of the tenets in this book. It's a great site focused on investing and building wealth.

Club Thrifty – Holly and Greg were able to ditch their 9-to-5 jobs after learning to manage their money. The blog focuses on ways to spend smartly, cut debt and earn extra income.

Bible Money Matters – Peter hits all the topics in personal finance but he also talks about faith and family. It's a great blog that will help you lead an inspired life.

Made in the USA
Middletown, DE
19 May 2022